More books by Taylor A
all available on Ama

All are blank notebooks, including *Things I Can't Say Out Loud in Meetings*, which also has fun quotes to keep you going through those endless meetings... Ideal gag gifts for work friends, or Secret Santa ideas for coworkers and even your boss!

Things
I Can't
Say
Out
Loud
In
Meetings

What My
Job Description
Says
Versus
What I
Actually
Do

Yes, I am
Amazing ✓
Brilliant at
my job ✓
A FREAKIN'
miracle
worker ✓

Contrary To
Popular Belief,
My To-Do List
Doesn't
Automatically
Include
Everyone Else's

Amazingly
Awesome
Ideas, Plans
&
Coping
Mechanisms
To Stay
Sane
At Work

Before we begin, this book is all about having fun and sharing laughs, not offering professional advice.

While we've put every effort into making the content entertaining and appropriate, we can't guarantee it's flawless. This book is eclectic...like the quotes within it.

The author and publishers are not responsible for any misinterpretations or mishaps that may arise from reading this book. Enjoy the sarcasm, irony and humor, and keep in mind that we're all about fun, not facts!

Welcome to Snarky Work Affirmations

...because sometimes the only thing keeping you from flipping your desk is a well-timed eye-roll and a passive-aggressive mantra.

As someone who's survived the joys of open-plan offices, endless meetings that fill up your calendar so you've no time to do anything else, and bosses who think a "quick favor" means "redo this entire project", I've created this tongue-in-cheek book so you can get through the day with flair and sarcasm.

If you've ever been volunteered for a task that isn't in your job description, watched technology malfunction moments before a deadline, or smiled through your 47th "quick sync", this is for you.

These affirmations, quotes, interactive pages, and more won't fix your workload, stop the calendar invites, or make the printer work, but they will help you release your inner snark. It's not therapy, but it is cheaper and won't get flagged by HR.

Think of it as emotional support, full of sarcasm, to enrich your internal monologue.

Use it to survive your day, one snarky thought at a time...

Taylor A. Wilde

How is Inner Sarcasm a Form of Self-Care?

Inner sarcasm can be a subtle but surprisingly powerful form of self-care when used mindfully...

Mental Distance from Stress
Inner sarcasm lets you mock your stressors internally – a kind of emotional buffer.

Instead of internalizing a negative event ("Wow, I'm such a failure"), you might think:
"Oh great, another stellar moment in my highlight reel."

This ironic framing gives you a psychological distance from distress, reducing its emotional grip.

Reduces the Pressure to Be Perfect
Sarcastic self-talk, when not cruel, can undercut perfectionism.

"Oh sure, I was definitely going to solve all my work problems by 5 p.m."

By poking fun at unrealistic expectations, you're more likely to accept imperfection and move on rather than spiral. It also helps you laugh at the chaos instead of absorbing it.

A sarcastic thought like "Not sure overnight miracles are part of my job description..." highlights the absurdity.

It's not giving up – it's letting go of unrealistic expectations.

How is Inner Sarcasm a Form of Self-Care?

Channeling Humor for Emotional Regulation
Sarcasm, even if dry or dark, engages your sense of humor.

And humor activates dopamine and endorphins, which reduce stress. It's a way of saying to yourself:
"This sucks, but at least I can laugh at it, if not about it."

Validation Without Pity
Inner sarcasm acknowledges that something is annoying, unfair, or difficult – without falling into self-pity.

It's validating, but with a sharp edge:
"Ah yes, because nothing screams 'life under control' like crying in the car over a spreadsheet."
That tone helps you vent while keeping your dignity intact.

Caution
It only works as self-care when it's aimed at situations, not at degrading yourself. There's a fine line between self-deprecating and self-destructive sarcasm.

Summary
Inner sarcasm is like giving yourself a side-eye and a smirk instead of a meltdown. When used skillfully, it's a mental strategy that can deflate anxiety, soften perfectionism, and help you laugh just enough to keep going.

I WELCOME CHALLENGES
THAT ARE URGENT, UNDEFINED, AND UNDER-RESOURCED, WHICH APPLY TO THE MAJORITY...

Helping You Pretend to Care Since 9 A.M.

(Fake it 'til you clock off)

Three meetings, four sighs, and one overly eager "Let's circle back" later, you've perfected the concerned head tilt, the strategic "Hmm…" and the sacred mute button.
You may not care – but you look amazing pretending. Gold star.
Now go forth and respond to nonsense with professional nodding and internal monologues, which could include some of these…

- I give 110% – mostly in facial expressions.
- I actively listen while mentally grocery shopping.
- I nod with purpose and pray no one asks for a follow-up.
- I radiate calm, mainly because I've given up.
- I am committed to excellence…until lunch.
- I don't rise to every challenge. Some I sidestep entirely.
- I maintain healthy boundaries by disappearing after every meeting.
- I am empowered by the illusion of autonomy.
- I'm not disengaged – I'm selectively involved.
- I log in with hope and log out with relief.
- I welcome back-to-back meetings as a chance to practice staying conscious.
- I've earned this paycheck with emotional restraint and strategic eye contact.

IN TEAM BRAINSTORMS, I EMBRACE

_____

_____

What I really mean...

I
welcome
every
new
initiative
with the
cautious
optimism
of
déjà vu

HR-Filtered Affirmations for Emotionally Exhausted Employees

Here are some affirmations to help you survive the office grind without completely losing your cool. These HR-friendly mantras are perfect for when you're emotionally drained but still need to keep it together – just barely.

Manifesting calm while plotting my escape...

- I am deeply committed to pretending everything is fine.
- I am a master of managing my stress...until 5 p.m.
- Today, I will successfully fake enthusiasm at every meeting.
- I am at peace with the fact that my inbox will never be empty.
- I excel at remaining calm while silently planning my exit strategy.
- I am an expert in smiling through the chaos.
- Today, I will pretend to care about my 50th email reminder.
- I am not just surviving; I am barely managing in style.
- I trust that coffee will solve all of my problems.
- I am perfectly content pretending my workload is reasonable.

I CHERISH TO-DO LISTS AS OPTIMISTIC FICTION

Doodle Time:
Passive-Aggressive Zen Sketch Page

Your coping mechanism disguised as creative expression...

—————— ● ——————

Draw a spiral that represents your growing to-do list, which will undoubtedly be a swirling black hole of tasks, requests, and "quick favors".

I
express
myself
clearly –
especially
through
passive-
aggressive
punctuation

INBOX
MOOD TRACKER

---●---

☐ I'm ready to tackle it.

☐ I'm afraid to look at it.

☐ I'm mentally calculating how long I can feasibly ignore it.

☐ I'm numb at this point.

☐ I resent its existence.

OTHER FEELINGS

_____

_____

_____

_____

_____

I MAINTAIN
BOUNDARIES
BY NEVER
ANSWERING EMAILS
BEFORE 9 A.M.
OR
AFTER 4:59 P.M.

Mindful Breathing for the Modern Employee

———— • ————

Inhale patience, exhale professional detachment. This exercise is your reminder that you don't have to absorb the chaos – you just have to sit near it while looking calm.

Whether you're mentally escaping a status meeting or avoiding a group chat meltdown, these corporate breathing cues will guide you to a place of near-stability.

———— • ————

Breathe in: I acknowledge the nonsense.

Breathe out: But I will not engage.

Breathe in: Serenity...or something like it.

Breathe out: Let the passive-aggression wash over me.

Repeat until your email notification dings.

Then clench internally and smile externally.

I FIND PEACE
IN PRETENDING TO
LOOK BUSY
WHILE
COMPLETELY
DISSOCIATING

I ENJOY HEARING "LET'S CIRCLE BACK ON THAT" BECAUSE

_____

_____

What I really mean...

I appreciate direction, even when it changes every 14 minutes

Micromanaged & Thriving (Barely) (For when "autonomy" is just a buzzword)

Whether you're thriving under constant supervision – or at least pretending to – or ever been looped in, copied in unnecessarily, or given "gentle reminders" five times a day.

Here, we celebrate the resilient few who manage to do their jobs with three managers, two trackers, and zero trust.

Because sometimes, the only autonomy you get is deciding whether to cry before or after the morning meeting.

- I take pride in doing my job twice – once on my own, once to make my manager feel involved.
- I trust the process – even when it's just someone hovering over my shoulder.
- I am capable, but monitored – like a very professional toddler.
- I value feedback, especially when it's the same note, phrased 23 different ways.
- I radiate independence while being cc'd on every email known to mankind.
- I welcome input, as long as it's repeated hourly.
- I'm empowered to make decisions – as long as I have to get six approvals first.

Micromanaged & Thriving (Barely) (For when "autonomy" is just a buzzword) ctd...

- I thrive in chaos. Especially chaos caused by 12 contradictory instructions.
- I appreciate being trusted with tasks, but not outcomes.
- I am grateful for my manager's support. All 117 daily check-ins of it.
- I am not overthinking – I'm just trying to remember which version of the instructions we're using today.
- I adapt well to change. Especially when it's someone changing my work immediately.
- I may not be autonomous, but I am still impressive – like a goldfish that's learned to tap dance.
- I succeed despite the micromanagement. Or maybe because I've surrendered to it. Hard to say.
- Micromanagement really brings out the passive in my aggressive.
- My workflow is a delicate dance between initiative and immediate correction.
- I'm efficiently over-instructed on a daily basis.

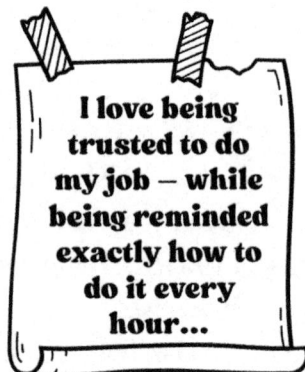

I love being trusted to do my job — while being reminded exactly how to do it every hour...

MICROMANAGEMENT SURVIVAL LOG

— • —

- ☐ Smiled and nodded while doing it my way

- ☐ Started to use corporate buzzwords as camouflage

- ☐ Added everything to a spreadsheet for plausible deniability

- ☐ Created fake task to distract my micromanager

- ☐ Implemented all feedback... into my mental "Nope" folder

SURVIVAL NOTES

_____

_____

_____

_____

_____

Sketch Therapy: Where Repressed Rage Meets Artistic Flair

Emotional survival, but make it artsy...

---•---

**Doodle your productivity graph today.
You probably had a strong start, then it
plunged after lunch, and there's a heroic
attempt to look busy until 5 p.m.
Bonus points for dramatic dips and snack-
related spikes.**

EVERY SPREADSHEET I FINISH IS A SILENT SCREAM INTO THE CORPORATE VOID

Smiling Through the Spreadsheet

(For Excel users and existential crisis survivors alike)

There's nothing like the calming cells of a spreadsheet to distract you from your slow spiral into corporate despair...

Whether you're battling pivot tables, wrestling with #REF! errors from deleted cells, deciphering #VALUE! when Excel just...refuses, or confronting a circular reference warning that loops through your last ounce of patience, these are for you.

Because sometimes, the only thing holding you together is...conditional formatting.

- I am in control...at least of this one cell.
- Every formula I type delays a meltdown.
- I align my values...and my columns.
- Today's chaos is neatly color-coded.
- I sort my data better than my emotions.
- I may not feel productive today, but at least my cells are locked.
- My future is unclear, but this filter isn't.
- I am one VLOOKUP away from snapping.
- Merge cells, not expectations.
- At least my formulas know what they're doing.
- I format cells with more care than my life.
- CTRL+S is the only thing holding me together.
- This spreadsheet is organized — unlike the rest of my workload.
- I trust the process...until #DIV/0! happens.
- Dragging formulas down, just like my mood.
- I balance spreadsheets better than my work-life balance.

I
love learning
new software...
especially
when it
replaces
something
that
already
worked

HR EMAILS ABOUT "WORK-LIFE BALANCE" MEAN

Modern Office Life
Where Sarcasm Is a Coping Strategy and Eye-Rolls Count as Cardio

For anyone who's sighed at an email, questioned a meeting, or stared blankly at a frozen screen – here's your daily dose of workplace truth bombs, served with eyebrow raises, a forced inane grin, and a stifled sigh of exasperation...

- If it takes more than one email to explain, it's not my problem.
- Another meeting? Excellent. Let's waste even more time together.
- My resting face is set to "please stop talking".
- Team bonding is just code for forced small talk and snack regrets.
- I value teamwork. From a safe emotional distance.
- If I had a swear jar at work, I'd be bankrupt.
- Every time someone says "urgent", a part of me dies.
- Every strategic plan is just a PowerPoint presentation dressed as chaos.
- If my computer freezes one more time, I will break some sort of record.
- I cherish my coworkers the same way I cherish pop-up ads and cookie consents.
- Every system update is an invitation to chaos.
- The more tabs I open, the closer I am to enlightenment – or a breakdown.
- Technology is amazing. Until you need it.
- No one can disturb my peace, unless they book a meeting.

I PROTECT MY PEACE BY AGGRESSIVELY CLOSING ALL TABS AT 5 P.M.

TASK AVOIDANCE TACTICS

———— • ————

☐ **Reorganized the paperclips**

☐ **Did a deep dive on chair ergonomics**

☐ **Scheduled a meeting to avoid doing actual work**

☐ **Tried to manifest productivity**

☐ **Other: _____**

AVOIDANCE JUSTIFICATION NOTES

_____

_____

_____

_____

I'm emotionally stable... as long as no one talks to me

Artful Avoidance: Your Daily Stress Relief...in Doodle Form

Quietly unraveling – one sketch at a time...

—————— ● ——————

Design your "mental storage box" and label it "Things I Pretend to Care About".
Let's be honest, some things at work are mentally filed straight under "smile and nod", so include all the tasks, updates, and conversations you pretend to care about. Make it fancy, make it overflowing, make it sarcastically color-coded.

Still Employed: A Celebration of Low Standards

(You didn't get fired – congrats?)

There's a special kind of excellence in doing just enough to not get fired. Not more, not less – just that sweet, legally ambiguous middle ground where performance reviews become vague compliments like "consistent" or "reliable presence".

You might not be the star, but you've mastered the art of survival via semi-frequent replies and the occasional "per my last email".

While others burn out chasing gold stars and growth plans, you're out here setting healthy boundaries by answering team messages at a glacial pace.

You don't overachieve – you exist at a sustainable hum of effort. The motto is "It's fine".

Being still employed isn't a miracle – it's a testament to well-timed head nods and enduring apathy.

You've weathered layoffs, reorganizations, and at least one team-building escape room. You didn't stand out, and that's what kept you in.

Celebrate yourself. You're not unemployed, and in this economy, that's practically a promotion.

I
will
not
engage
in
petty drama...
unless
it's
really good

OFFICE ZEN-ISH
MOCKERY IN EVERY BLANK SPACE

Because your sarcastic sense of humor aids your inner peace...

———— ● ————

I am _____ about today's

_____ because my _____

is already _____.

*

I bring _____ to every

meeting, even if my _____

_____ is screaming "no".

*

My motivation is _____,

my patience is _____, and my last

nerve is _____.

*

Every time I hear the word "_____",

I feel a deep _____ in my

_____.

I CELEBRATE SMALL WINS, LIKE AVOIDING THAT ONE COWORKER ALL DAY

MORE OFFICE ZEN-ISH MOCKERY IN EVERY BLANK SPACE

Because your sarcastic sense of humor aids your inner peace…

———————— • ————————

I'm manifesting _____,

and inner _____,

but mostly I'm just waiting for _____.

*

Today's plan is to _____

until someone notices, and then _____

_____ when they don't,

and reward myself with _____.

*

With every email, I gain _____,

lose _____, and channel my inner

_____.

*

My superpower is smiling while mentally _____

_____ through another

_____.

I remain
calm
knowing
"circling back"
is
just
corporate
for
"you failed me"

"Things I Definitely Don't Think About at Work"

A mock mindfulness list
that's anything but mindful...

- Whether pretending to take notes counts as multitasking.
- If I can write a resignation letter in just emojis.
- How much longer I can fake enthusiasm before it becomes a health hazard.
- If anyone else is as emotionally allergic to group chats as I am.
- How many deadlines I can dodge before HR gets involved.
- How many "quick questions" break a person.
- Whether I can expense therapy as a team-building activity.
- If I stare hard enough, will the printer fix itself?
- If responding to emails in my dreams counts as overtime.
- How many spreadsheets it takes to trigger an existential crisis.
- Whether anyone else is googling "how to look engaged in meetings".
- If passive-aggressive calendar invites are an art form.
- How to make eye contact on Zoom without looking like a serial killer.
- If pretending to understand the assignment counts as doing it.
- If anyone noticed I've been in "Do Not Disturb" mode for three days.
- If opening my inbox counts as a daily act of bravery.

I FIND CLARITY IN CHAOS – ESPECIALLY THE KIND I DIDN'T CAUSE

TODAY'S OFFICE ENERGY LEVEL

—— • ——

☐ Going for it, eventually

☐ Meh at best

☐ Thankful for the mute button

☐ Low, but coffee helps

☐ Gradually powering down

NOTES FOR FUTURE REFERENCE

_____

_____

_____

_____

_____

Do It Yourself
Doodle Page

No expectations. No deadlines.
Just your pen and passive resistance...

I
write emails
that are
clear,
concise,
and
loaded with
subtle
contempt

Affirmation Mantra:
The Power of
Selective Indifference

---●---

**Sometimes the healthiest move at work
is caring less – strategically.**

**When your "give-a-damn" is broken but meetings and
deadlines keep coming, selective indifference
becomes emotional efficiency.**

**You don't need to fix every problem, join every
discussion, or respond to every email with soul-
crushing enthusiasm.**

**Just breathe, say "noted", and zone out with
professional eye contact.**

---●---

I release what I cannot fix.

I ignore what I cannot care about.

I acknowledge that "noted"
is a valid emotional response.

I am centered. I am unbothered.

I am already halfway to logging off.

I TRUST THAT "QUICK CALL?" MEANS A FULL HOUR OF MISCOMMUNICATION

I LOOK FORWARD TO A "QUICK" SYNC THAT RUNS 45 MINUTES OVER BECAUSE

_____

_____

What I really mean...

I will manifest peace... right after I finish muttering insults under my breath

Getting Through the Daily Grind
(With an Internal Sigh
and a Muffled Groan)

In every workplace, there's a fine art to showing up, staying composed, and finding humor in the mayhem.
This collection of tongue-in-cheek affirmations celebrates the unspoken truths of office life – from the performance of productivity to the quiet triumph of making it through the day...

- I trust that one day my job will make sense. Today is not that day.
- I am mentally clocked out, but I show up like a pro.
- I welcome challenges, especially when they're someone else's fault.
- I will complete my tasks with grace, bitterness, and mild eye-rolling.
- I believe in doing my best, unless it requires effort.
- I face each task with quiet dread and expert fake enthusiasm.
- I'm not behind – I'm just working at a pace that confuses time.
- I am grateful for my job, and equally grateful when it's over each day.
- I lead with empathy – towards myself for showing up.
- I manifest inner peace by mentally rehearsing my resignation speech.
- I am confident in my ability to look busy without actually doing anything.

I VALUE TEAMWORK, PARTICULARLY WHEN SOMEONE ELSE VOLUNTEERS FIRST

Pen, Paper, Peace (and a sprinkle of silent judgment)

Your inner meltdown in aesthetically pleasing form...

———————— ● ————————

Write a calming affirmation in bubble letters. Whether it's "This is fine", "Breathe in, log out", or "I get paid for this?", make it big, make it bold, and pretend it's helping.

I
accept
that
"urgent"
just
means
someone
didn't
plan

Meeting Bingo

Let's not reinvent the wheel	Win-win situation	To your point...	Drill down into the data
Synergy	It is what it is...	Touch base	On the same page
We need to be agile	Let's sync up	Let's unpack that	Value-add
Can we all agree?	At the end of the day...	I don't have anything to add	Let's circle back on that

Actions for Future Reference

_____
_____
_____
_____
_____

CORPORATE NUMBNESS: BREATHE IN, BURN OUT

A meditation for mid-meeting meltdowns

———————— ● ————————

Breathe in that stale office air...the one filled with endless emails, pointless meetings, and the faint hum of the copier in the corner.
Hold it in. Let it slowly strangle your soul.

Now, exhale...but not too loud. You don't want to interrupt someone explaining their "thoughts" on the latest "synergy" initiative.

Repeat this process for the rest of the meeting, until you've mastered the art of looking like you're paying attention while absorbing only the essential details.

Stay present, but keep your responses brief. Nod occasionally, avoid unnecessary commentary, and keep your escape plan on standby for when the meeting finally ends.

I RISE ABOVE THE DRAMA, MOSTLY BY STAYING QUIET
WHEN ISSUES ARE HIGHLIGHTED IN TEAM UPDATES

ALWAYS HAPPY TO BE IN A MEETING THAT COULD'VE BEEN AN EMAIL BECAUSE

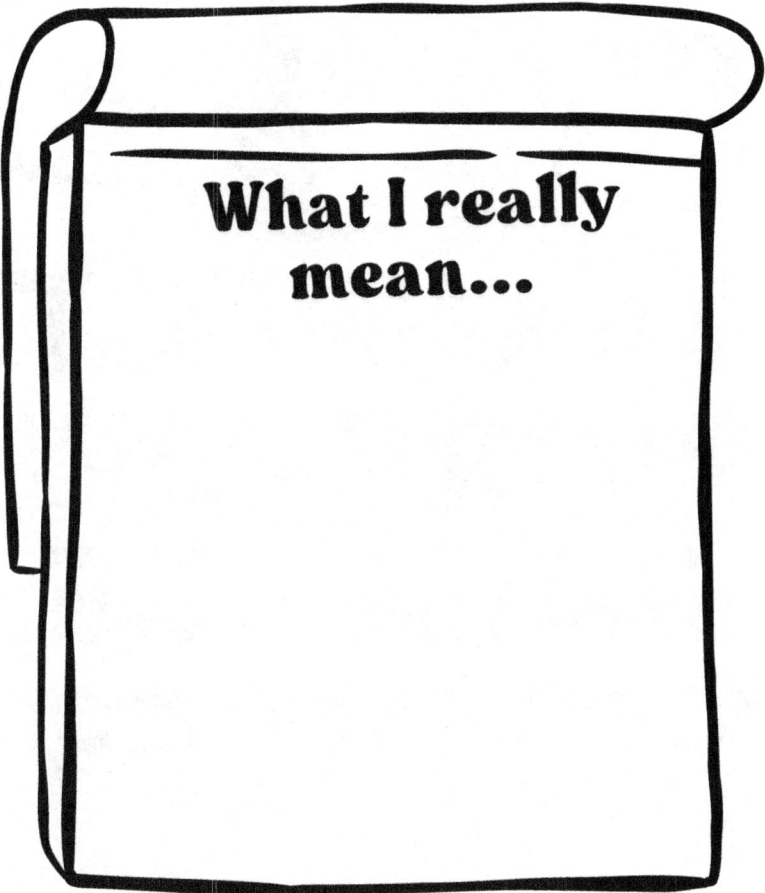

_____

_____

What I really mean...

I RESPECT WORK-LIFE BALANCE, MOSTLY IN THEORY

A DEDICATED SECTION FOR MEETING JARGON AND CLICHÉS *WITH THEIR SARCASTIC TRANSLATIONS...*

Because we've all been there...
on numerous occasions...

Meeting Jargon and Clichés
and their sarcastic translations...

"Let's circle back on that."

Let's pretend we'll revisit this, then never speak of it again.

"Drill down into the data."

Please find the one number that supports my argument.

"Low-hanging fruit."

Let's do the bare minimum and feel accomplished.

Meeting Jargon and Clichés
and their sarcastic translations...

"Think outside the box."

Please say something wild so we can immediately reject it.

"Synergy."

Buzzword that makes us sound like we know what we're doing.

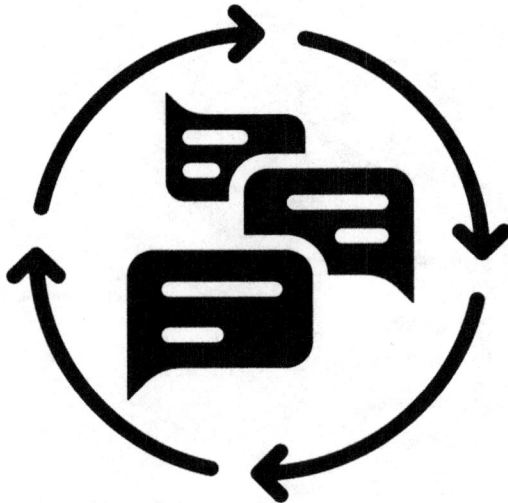

"Touch base."

Just enough contact to tick a box, but not to solve anything.

"At the end of the day..."

I'm about to say something vague but conclusive.

"Value-add."

I'm not sure what this does, but I hope it looks useful.

"Let's put a pin in it."

Let's forget this ever happened.

"It is what it is."

I've given up, and so should you.

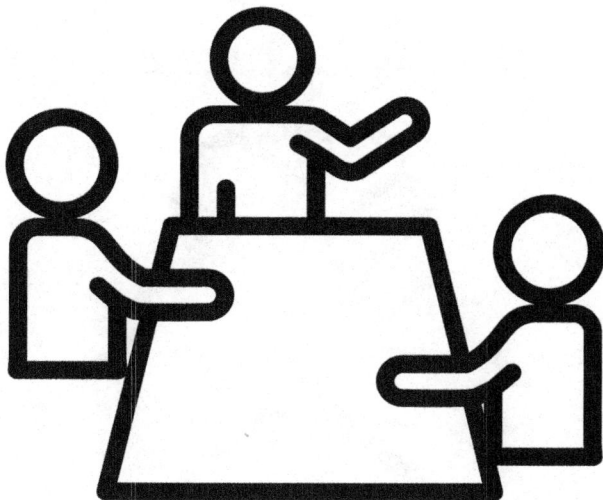

"Bandwidth" (as in "Do you have the bandwidth?")

I want you to do more work, but nicely.

"Can we take this offline?"

I'd rather not have witnesses for this awkward conversation.

"On the same page."

I need everyone to pretend they understand this.

"Circle the wagons."

Something went wrong, and now we panic as a group.

"Let's not reinvent the wheel."

I don't want to think too hard today.

PLAN

"Level-set expectations."

Let me lower your hopes in a formal way.

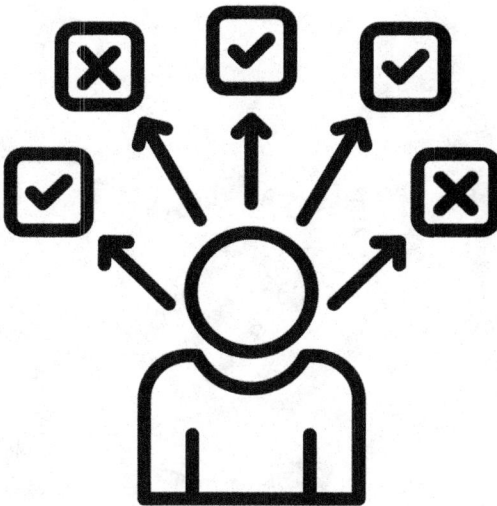

"Win-win situation."

You'll work more; I'll get the credit.

"Run it up the flagpole."

Let's throw this out there and see who dares to object.

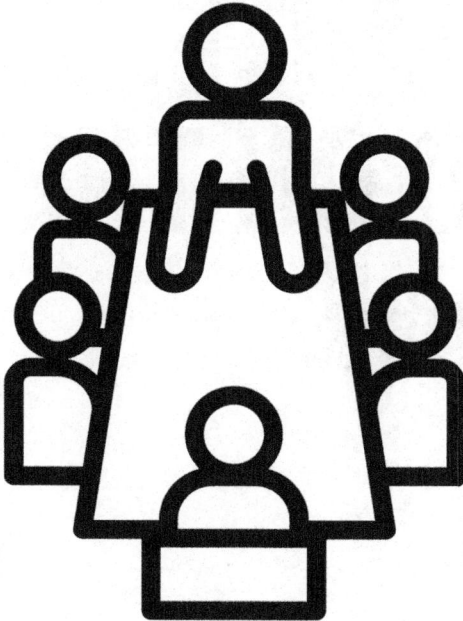

I SHOW UP EVERY DAY— ON TIME, ON MUTE, AND ON THE BRINK

Guided Visualization: "The Meeting That Got Cancelled"

---•---

Welcome to the happiest place in the workplace: the moment a meeting gets cancelled.

This guided visualization is your permission slip to emotionally detach and spiritually snack.

For just a few glorious seconds, there are no agendas, no action items – just the pure, unfiltered bliss of unexpected freedom.

---•---

Close your eyes. Imagine you receive a calendar notification.

It says: "Meeting Cancelled".

You feel joy. You feel light.

You feel the overwhelming urge to go get snacks and do absolutely nothing with the time you just got back.

This is your safe space. Return here as needed.

I LOVE IT WHEN SOMEONE SENDS A CALENDAR INVITE WITHOUT CONTEXT— MYSTERY IS EXCITING

I LOOK FORWARD TO

_____

_____

IN MEETINGS

What I really mean...

_____

_____

_____

_____

_____

_____

I'm
not
antisocial...
I'm
selectively
social
with
an
escape
plan

Meetings That Could've Been Avoided: Notes from the Void

Because someone thought they were necessary

- I trust that no one else read the agenda either.
- I welcome alignment meetings to realign from last week's alignment.
- I am fully present in this meeting, at least until the third bullet point.
- I maintain eye contact and suppress all visible panic.
- I delegate responsibility by pretending I thought someone else was handling it.
- I choose calm over confrontation...mostly to avoid follow-up meetings.
- I trust in my ability to make things look done (usually by winging it).
- I contribute value by repeating what someone else just said.
- I achieve clarity by nodding until the topic changes.
- I demonstrate initiative by pretending I understood that vague request.
- I find purpose in creating action items I will immediately forget.
- I am grateful for vague updates I can't question.
- I remain calm, even when someone says "let's circle back offline".
- I ground myself through passive-aggressive note-taking.
- I stay engaged by mentally designing my resignation letter.
- I show leadership by asking questions no one wanted answered.

I FIND JOY IN WATCHING SHARED SCREENS NAVIGATE CHAOS IN REAL TIME

Virtual Meeting Bingo

"Can you repeat that?"	Someone says "Can you all see my screen?"	"Can we take this offline?"	A dog or child appears on camera
Someone talks over another person	"I'll send the details in an email"	"That's a great question"	"Next slide please"
The speaker's mic is on mute	"Can everyone hear me?"	Random noise interrupts call	"Let's table this for now"
"I think we're all on the same page"	At least one person's camera freezes	"Sorry, you're breaking up"	"I'll follow up on that"

Actions for Future Reference

_____

_____

_____

_____

Zen Thoughts from Someone Who's Already Emotionally Checked Out

(Be here now...or at least until 5 p.m.)

I radiate calm because I no longer care.

I participate just enough to not get flagged.

Letting go daily.

I no longer fight the chaos — I spectate.

I'm trying to avoid eye contact responsibly.

Mute. Smile. Survive.

I'm productive in theory, exhausted in practice.

Calm. Detached. Paid.

I value alignment — between my body and the exit.

Floating through deadlines.

I believe in rest...mostly during meetings.

I show up, zone out, and log off.

I find purpose in pretending to look busy.

Inbox, not insight.

I listen intently while mentally thinking about my evening meal.

Zen Thoughts from Someone Who's Already Emotionally Checked Out

(Be here now...or at least until 5 p.m.)

Smiling through apathy.

I let go of what I never cared about.

I trust the process. Just not the people in charge of it.

Here. But only physically.

I practice stillness, mostly by ignoring notifications.

Accept. Numb. Repeat.

Quietly floating towards the weekend.

Here for the salary.

I engage with work like I engage with spam emails.

I treat every meeting like a screensaver: low movement, no input.

Calmly ignoring everything with purpose.

Surrender to autopilot.

Serenity through strategic emotional withdrawal.

Caring takes effort.

At peace with doing less.

IT'S EMPOWERING WHEN MY OWN IDEA IS EXPLAINED BACK TO ME BECAUSE

_____

_____

What I really mean...

I

am

emotionally

available –

after

5 p.m.

and

with

wine

Affirmations for When "Quitting" Isn't Financially Viable

Because your financial outgoings don't care about your burnout.

- I'm not thriving, but my credit card appreciates the effort.
- I choose employment over inner peace. Bold.
- I stay motivated by bills I didn't choose.
- I show up for my salary, not my passion.
- I fuel my burnout to uphold my financial decisions.
- I am not trapped – I'm just fiscally committed.
- I accept the stress I cannot afford to escape.
- I don't love my job, but I do love buying

- I suppress emotions until payday, then repeat.
- I work to live, but mostly to pay my bills.
- I can't walk away, but I can emotionally ghost.
- I do what I love – when I'm off the clock.
- I trade my time for money – and trauma.
- I survive on salary, sarcasm, and occasional snacks.
- I am committed to this salary more than myself.
- I budget time, money, and emotional breakdowns wisely.
- I can't quit now – I just ordered a new

- I grind so I can afford a few minutes of joy.
- I radiate endurance. Mostly financial. Definitely not emotional.
- I sacrifice inner peace for my monthly salary. Namaste-ish.

REASONS I'M NOT RESPONDING TO THAT EMAIL

and what I should say out loud

— • —

- ☐ **I've already answered this.**
  As per my previous email.

- ☐ **I'm not a magician.**
  I'll do my best to address this.

- ☐ **I'm embracing selective reading.**
  I'll review it, thank you for the insights.

- ☐ **I just don't want to.**
  I'll put it on my to-do list.

- ☐ **It's not that urgent.**
  I'll get to it when I'm able.

- ☐ **I have no energy left for polite replies.**
  Thank you for your patience.

I
treat
my
unread emails
like my
emotions...
ignored
until it's
a crisis

Do It Yourself
Doodle Page

**Because HR frowns on what
you really want to say....**

I Hope This Email Finds You Miserable Too

(Motivation for the modern inbox martyr.)

I type with intention.
Reread with rage.
And hit "send" with the full force of suppressed fury.

May my polite tone confuse you.
My punctuation unsettle you.
And my cc list haunt you.

I don't rise and grind – I log in and tolerate.
Each "hope you're well" is a battle cry.
Each "quick follow-up" chips at my soul.
And yet, I reply...professionally.

Every email is an opportunity,
To say what I really think...
And then delete it, reword it, and add a smiley face.

I write "just checking in",
But I mean: "respond before I lose my last shred of sanity".
Ah, the poetry of corporate communication.

Inbox zero is a myth.
Inner peace is a lie.
But I'm still here, cc'd into oblivion.
Holding it together with drafts and deep sighs.

Every "reply to all" is an attack on my soul

I LOVE BEING CC'D ON A 30-EMAIL THREAD BECAUSE

_____

_____

What I really mean...

Snarky Quotes as a Pick-Me-Up to Get Through the Daily Grind

Work can feel more like a comedy show than a job. These sarcastic affirmations highlight the quirks of office life with a healthy dose of irony. From endless meetings to mysterious "work styles", these affirmations remind you that you're not alone in the chaos.

9-to-5 Irony

- I cherish the daily opportunity to answer questions already answered in emails.
- I feel seen whenever someone takes credit for my idea.
- I love how some people confuse confidence with competence.
- I thrive in open-plan offices – who doesn't love ambient chewing, slurping, and oversharing?
- I respect everyone's unique work style, even the one that involves doing nothing.
- I admire the consistency of my coworkers' 4:59 p.m. crises.
- I love how "collaborative" projects reveal everyone's true personalities.
- I trust that someone will eventually learn how the printer works.
- I'm amazed by the talent required to appear busy for eight hours straight.
- I enjoy when "quick questions" become full therapy sessions.

I
appreciate
my
coworkers'
quirks
while
silently
cataloging
them

THE GRATITUDE LIST (OFFICE EDITION)

*A fill-in-the-blank journaling section
for your most
insincere workplace thankfulness*

———————— • ————————

I guess I should be grateful for _____

_____

I'm contractually obligated to appreciate _____

_____

I'm clinging to the silver lining of _____

_____

I've been told to be thankful for _____

_____

I'm spiritually tolerating _____

_____

I pretend to value _____

_____

I'm surviving thanks to _____

_____

I AM GRATEFUL FOR THE SALARY, NOT NECESSARILY THE WORK REQUIRED TO EARN IT

THE GRATITUDE LIST (OFFICE EDITION)

*A fill-in-the-blank journaling section
for your most
insincere workplace thankfulness ctd...*

———————— ● ————————

I whisper "thanks" through gritted teeth for _____

_____

I express mild, exhausted gratitude for _____

_____

I begrudgingly acknowledge the existence of _____

_____

I offer a slow clap of appreciation for _____

_____

I tolerate with a hint of gratitude _____

_____

I nod politely at the idea of being thankful for _____

_____

I'm emotionally numb but technically thankful for ____

_____

I
have exactly
enough
energy
to
appear
productive
and
nothing more

Creative Outburst Page: Express Yourself...Without Getting Fired

When venting isn't allowed, draw instead...

———————— ● ————————

Draw a brain with Post-it notes.
Your head is full of deadlines, drama, and corporate survival scripts, and don't forget those reminders, fake enthusiasm, and emotional buffering.
One to start you off could be "Smile, they're watching" – nothing says "thriving" like masking existential dread with a professional grin.

PROFESSIONAL-ISH – SHOWING UP IS HALF THE REGRET

(Because trying is optional.)

I wandered in close enough to being on time.

I gave it my least, and that's just fine.

I looked pretty focused, at least from afar.

I kept a straight face while I lowered the bar.

I'd try a bit harder, but that sounds like work.

I'm proud that I managed not to go berserk.

I can't say I excelled, but I kept any drama at bay.

My vibe was "present", and that's enough for today.

I
love
when
people
"loop me in"
right
before
things
go
wrong

I

WHEN THE TEAM CELEBRATES FINISHING THE PROJECT I BASICALLY COMPLETED

What I really mean...

Staying Employed One Eye-Roll at a Time

(HR can't fire what they can't prove.)

It's a fine balance – doing just enough to stay off the radar while silently judging everything around you.

You show up (more or less on time), attend meetings (camera off and mic muted for as long as you can get away with it), and respond to emails (eventually).

Your true superpower? Eye-rolls so discreet they qualify as professional gestures.
You're not lazy – you're emotionally efficient.

You've survived surprise "quick chats" and being "volunteered" for projects you didn't even know about. You may not be thriving, but you're still on payroll, which is a miracle in itself.

Your enthusiasm? Strategically minimal.
Your productivity? Interpretive.
But your ability to endure nonsense with a blank stare and an open spreadsheet? Unmatched.

So, if you're navigating office life one sarcastic breath at a time, take heart. You're not alone.

Embrace the side-eye, lean into selective participation, and do whatever it takes to keep your sanity intact.

You don't have to love your job – you just have to outlast it, or at least until the next company restructure or AI takes over...

I
respect
everyone's
opinion,
especially
when
they
repeat
mine
louder

WORKPLACE MOOD TRACKER

Use as often as needed, or whenever you feel a strong urge to scream into your keyboard. Bonus points for consistency.

— ● —

- [ ] **Thriving (in denial)**
- [ ] **Holding it together with coffee and lies**
- [ ] **Emotionally out of office**
- [ ] **Functioning...technically**
- [ ] **Replying to emails I don't emotionally endorse**
- [ ] **Managing expectations downward**
- [ ] **One notification ping away from a dramatic career change**
- [ ] **Smiling through the office apocalypse that is my working life**

I PACE MYSELF TO AVOID GIVING ANYONE FALSE HOPE

Passive-Aggressive Art Zone: Because Your Stress Needs an Outlet

An artistic release for your workplace-induced spirals...

———————— • ————————

Design a trophy titled "Best at Acting Busy". If your talents include looking productive while muttering sarcasm and perfecting the eye-roll, this one's for you.
Honor your snarky hustle trophy with sparkles, gold trim, and flair – because your sarcasm deserves all the awards.

In the Office Backhanded Compliments You Wish You Could Say Out Loud...

You complicate things with such natural, effortless flair

You make bold choices – usually without good reason

You're a visionary – mostly of unfinished tasks

You communicate like no one's listening – thankfully

You're always unavailable – self-care goals, or something

You lead meetings straight into dead ends – effortlessly

You always show up – eventually, and unprepared

You always delegate problems with just the right tone

You're a team player, especially when credit's involved

Redirecting blame is your true professional superpower

You're great at making things worse with enthusiasm

You vanish mid-crisis – so calming, so inspiring

In the Office Backhanded Compliments You Wish You Could Say Out Loud ctd...

You inspire others...to find new jobs

You make ignoring problems look oddly strategic

Your time management keeps us guessing – constantly

Your confidence is completely unburdened by actual skill

Your leadership style is impressively hands-off and clueless

You deflect issues like it's your calling in life

You really have a talent for letting chaos build character

You bring such clarity...to absolutely no situation

You simplify everything by avoiding it entirely

Your ideas really challenge our will to care

You bring the drama, never the solution

You bring balance – mostly by doing nothing

I give 100% at work – spread unevenly across things I need to do each day

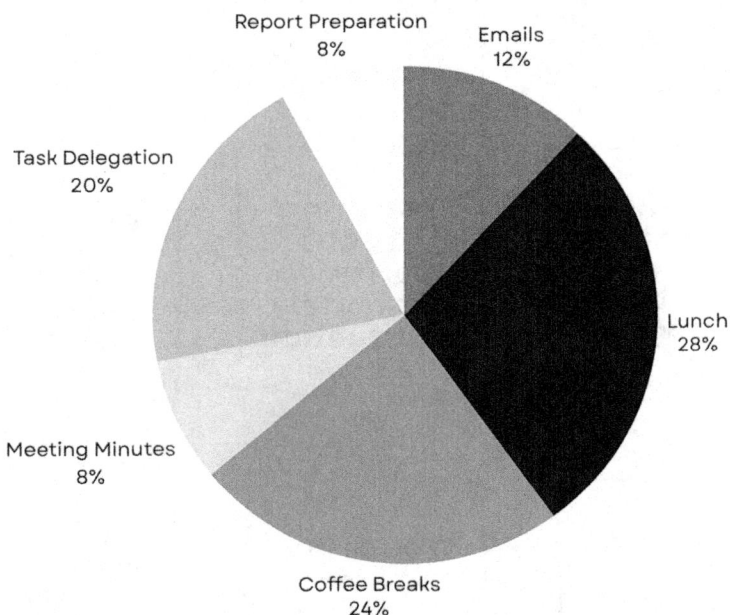

Pie chart:
- Report Preparation 8%
- Emails 12%
- Lunch 28%
- Coffee Breaks 24%
- Meeting Minutes 8%
- Task Delegation 20%

Because Screaming Before You Leave the House Isn't Sustainable

(This is your new coping mechanism. You're welcome.)

Sure, primal screaming into a towel used to help. But lately, even that can't compete with the daily avalanche of "quick chats", urgent-but-not-really emails, and meetings that feel like performance art.

You've tried deep breathing. You've even tried faking technical difficulties. At this point, your most realistic path to sanity is simply...lowering the bar.

Forget hustle. Embrace the warm, numbing comfort of quiet resignation. Channel your energy into controlled eye-rolls, well-timed "noted" replies, and looking extremely focused while doing absolutely nothing.

True peace is realizing you don't need to fix everything – especially when it's not even in your job description.

So skip the morning scream session. Sip your coffee. Let the chaos swirl around you like a corporate snow globe.

You're not giving up – you're emotionally optimizing.

IT'S GREAT RECEIVING CALENDAR INVITES LABELED "OPTIONAL" BECAUSE

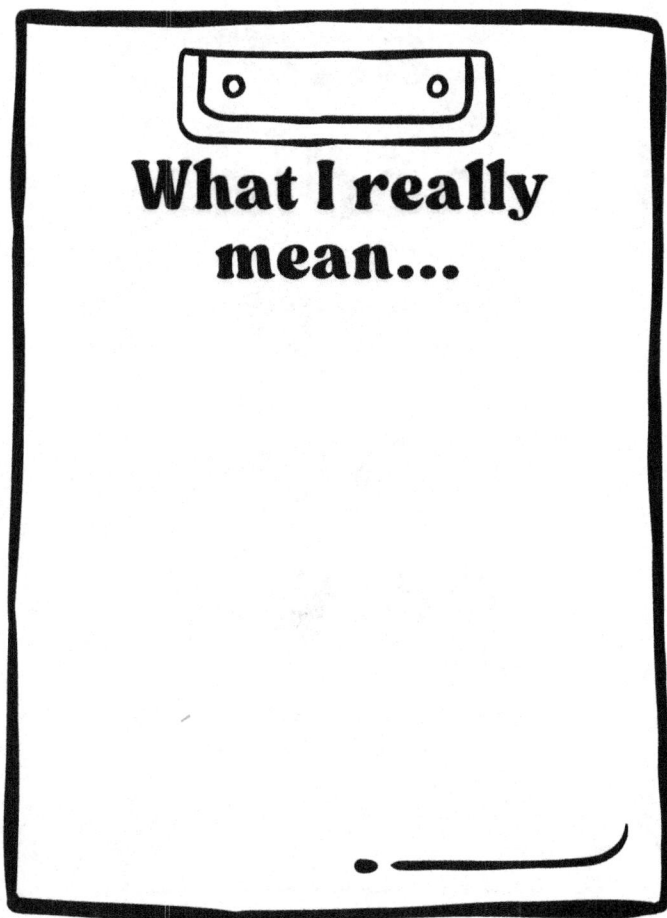

_____

_____

What I really mean...

I
love
waking
up
and
immediately
regretting
my
career
choices

Things I Say in My Head So I Don't Get Fired

Bite-sized sarcasm to fuel your polite, professional facade and add to your ongoing internal monologue...

- I am fine. Everything is fine. This is my fine face.
- I find inner strength every time I resist quitting via email.
- I know my worth – it's just not reflected in my job title.
- I trust that everything happens for a reason – usually budget cuts.
- I affirm my reality daily: I work, I suffer, I pretend to care.
- I am skilled at multitasking: appearing interested while zoning out.
- I love repeating myself because no one reads emails.
- Let me pretend to consider that.
- I bring toxic positivity to offset actual competence.
- Of course I have time to do your job too.
- Another last-minute request? My adrenaline needed a hit.
- No worries. I'll just manifest boundaries later.
- I'm just here for the salary and the printer only jams when it's urgent.
- My work ethic is directly proportional to how much coffee I've had and how much nonsense I've heard.

I DON'T
RISE AND SHINE.

I CAFFEINATE
AND
HOPE FOR
THE BEST.

TODAY'S PASSIVE-AGGRESSIVE VIBE

---•---

- [ ] I noticed that.

- [ ] "As per my last email..."

- [ ] Totally fine.

- [ ] No rush, I guess.

- [ ] I'll handle it. Again.

- [ ] Thanks for that.

- [ ] Sure, whatever.

CREATIVE EXCUSES FOR MISSING DEADLINES

_____

_____

_____

_____

_____

I will overcome every obstacle with the help of caffeine and quiet rage

Draw It Out: Quiet Rebellion, One Pen Stroke at a Time

Stress relief cleverly camouflaged as doodling...

———————— ● ————————

Create a calming "Mute Button" icon for
your soul – use mentally during calls.
Every call has that moment – the one where
you wish you could mute the entire situation,
not just your mic.
Use it mentally during meetings filled with
buzzwords, interruptions, or that coworker
overexplaining something.
Press internally. Repeat as needed.

Workplace Zen:
I Don't Care,
But Professionally...

(For inner peace in passive-aggression)

Inhale: I acknowledge the chaos.
Exhale: But that's not my department.

Inhale: I hear your feedback.
Exhale: I'm ignoring it with grace.

Inhale: I let go of the outcome.
Exhale: Because I never cared to begin with.

I am calm.
I am composed.
I am emotionally outsourced.

I am valued... but not *valuable* enough to get a lunch break before 3 p.m.

I RELISH A LAST-MINUTE "URGENT" REQUEST BECAUSE

_____

_____

What I really mean...

OK at Work:
The Bare Minimum Manifesto

Affirmations for Functioning-ish Adults

- I showed up. That's enough heroism for today.
- I give 100% – just not all at once.
- I bring value...mostly through sarcastic commentary.
- I am fully booked with pretending to be busy.
- I excel at responding to emails in my head.
- I am professionally present, emotionally out of office.
- I believe in doing my part – as long as it's the smallest part.
- I maintain a perfect balance of effort and avoidance.
- I schedule breaks like a pro. The work? That's negotiable.
- I don't chase promotions – I let them walk right past.
- I attend meetings with my camera off and judgment on.
- I keep my morale high by mentally spending the raise I'm never getting.
- I multitask by thinking about quitting while working.
- I am grateful for my paycheck and nothing else.
- I respond to "Can we chat?" like it's a threat.
- I radiate "please don't assign me anything" energy.

I COMMUNICATE CLEARLY, ESPECIALLY WHEN I'M PASSIVE-AGGRESSIVELY SLAMMING MY KEYBOARD

CORPORATE CALM
FOR THE CHAOTICALLY EMPLOYED

Tick your way to "peace" (or at least pretend).

- ☐ Ignored a calendar invite until it became irrelevant
- ☐ Said "Let's circle back" instead of screaming
- ☐ Pretended to take notes during a call
- ☐ Didn't cry in the bathroom—growth!
- ☐ Closed 12 tabs like a digital detox
- ☐ Smiled while internally drafting my resignation
- ☐ Breathed deeply (or at least sighed loudly)
- ☐ Replied "Thanks for the update" without punching a wall
- ☐ Remembered I'm not paid enough to care that much
- ☐ Survived another meeting that could've been a nap

I
radiate
competence,
especially
when
no one
asks
follow-up
questions

Zen-ish Scribbles:
Channel Your Workplace Feelings

Creative expression, secretly holding it all together...

———————— ● ————————

Draw a small plant and name it:
"My will to log on".
Some mornings, your motivation is thriving.
Most mornings, it's a wilted desk plant
hanging on by a leaf.
Is your plant sprouting with hope? Barely
alive? Propped up by caffeine and sarcasm?
Give it a name, give it a pot, and try not to let
it dry out before lunch.

Whispers of Positivity for the Overworked and Under-Caffeinated

(It's like therapy, but cheaper and <u>less</u> effective.)

You're doing great...at pretending to care.

One more task and you'll officially qualify for a medal in surviving nonsense.

You didn't aggressively scroll through job vacancies on LinkedIn today. Progress!

That's not burnout – it's just your soul quietly buffering.

Your inbox may be full, but so is your passive-aggression.

Remember: if you stay very still, maybe no one will assign you anything new.

Your coffee is working harder than your entire department.

You've survived 100% of your worst meetings so far. Barely.

Your enthusiasm may be fake, but your exhaustion is real.

Repeat after me: "I am not paid enough to panic."

SARCASTIC WORK AFFIRMATIONS
FILL-IN-THE-BLANK EDITION

Because nothing says emotional resilience like forced positivity with a side of sarcasm.

———————— ● ————————

I am fully prepared to pretend _____

_____ is fine.

Today, I choose to rise above _____

_____ and just mute it.

Especially when dealing with _____

_____ I radiate calm.

I give 110%...mostly to avoiding _____

_____.

I will approach _____

_____ with grace and passive aggression.

I find peace in knowing _____

_____ isn't my job.

I honor my limits by ignoring _____

_____ completely.

I THRIVE UNDER PRESSURE THAT COULD'VE BEEN AVOIDED WITH BASIC PLANNING AND COMMON SENSE

SARCASTIC WORK AFFIRMATIONS
FILL-IN-THE-BLANK EDITION

*Because nothing says emotional resilience
like forced positivity with a side of sarcasm ctd...*

———————— ● ————————

I accept what I cannot change – like _____

_____.

I find purpose in pretending _____

_____ is important.

I trust the process, even if _____

_____ is in charge.

I attract success and repel _____

_____ automatically.

I stay grounded, even while _____

_____ falls apart.

I give myself permission to ignore _____

_____ today.

I release the urge to fix _____

_____. Not my circus.

Toxic But Employed: Daily Affirmations for the Corporate Soul

(HR-UNapproved vibes only)

- I am a ray of sunshine...until I check my inbox.
- I bring good vibes and quiet resentment to every meeting.
- I smile not because I'm happy, but because HR is watching.
- I am calm, collected, and quietly documenting everything.
- I do not gossip – I participate in collaborative venting.
- I lead with kindness...unless I'm in a spreadsheet.
- I respect everyone's opinion, especially when it aligns with mine.
- I am grounded, centered, and ready to fake enthusiasm.
- I set boundaries. They are mostly emotional.
- I forgive, but I also take notes – just in case.
- I contribute meaningfully. Occasionally even during work hours.
- I manage stress by sharing memes and disappearing.
- I am the picture of grace under passive-aggressive pressure.
- I collaborate, communicate, and quietly judge.
- I trust the process...will eventually stop making everything worse.

Thank You for Reading Snarky Work Affirmations

Some final affirmations to tick off for surviving work by letting your inner sarcasm do the heavy lifting.

- [ ] I am productive in mysterious, undocumented ways...

- [ ] I grow professionally every time I clean up after someone's "strategic decision".

- [ ] I am focused, unless distracted by literally anything else...

- [ ] I follow orders...just very loosely and with a lot of internal commentary.

- [ ] I am not ignoring your message – I'm just prioritizing my inner peace.

- [ ] I will nod through this Zoom call like my brain isn't buffering.

- [ ] I maintain professionalism through forced detachment and deep breaths.

So, if you've made it this far without rage-quitting, congrats – that's peak professionalism.

Remember, in a world of endless meetings, vague feedback, and "collaborative" chaos, your sarcasm isn't just a coping mechanism – it's your superpower.

I hope these snarky affirmations have helped whenever workplace nonsense reached critical levels.

Stay snarky, stay unbothered, and above all keep smiling like you didn't just draft your resignation in your head...twice.

I
manage
expectations
with
vague
replies
and
strategic
silence...

Printed in Dunstable, United Kingdom